# STILL ALIVE

## NOTES FROM AUSTRALIA'S IMMIGRATION DETENTION SYSTEM

SAFDAR AHMED

D1560424

TWELVE

PANELS
PRESS

Part of this book was first published online by GetUp! in 2015 as *Villawood: Notes from an immigration detention centre*.

Publication of this work was supported by the School of Culture and Communication at the University of Melbourne.

First published in 2021

Twelve Panels Press
98 Collier Crescent, Brunswick West 3055, Victoria, Australia
www.twelvepanelspress.com

A catalogue record for this book is available from the National Library of Australia

ISBN 978 0 98059 3730

Cover design by Joanna Hunt
Text design by Safdar Ahmed and Joanna Hunt

Teachers' notes available from www.twelvepanelspress.com

Print and quality control in China by Tingleman Pty Ltd

10 9 8 7 6 5 4 3

www.safdarahmed.com

The publishers thank Pat Grant, Holly Jenkins, Hugh Crosthwaite, Belinda Bolliger, Joanna Hunt, Hilary Reynolds, Isobelle Carmody, Shaun Tan, David Manne, Ahmad Hakim, Adam Possamai, Kerry Robinson, Alfred Hornung and Lily Huang for invaluable support and advice.

# CONTENTS

*The consul banged the table and said,*

*'If you've got no passport you're officially dead':*

*But we are still alive, my dear, but we are still alive.*


W. H. Auden, 'Refugee Blues'

# VILLAWOOD

...is a largely industrial area some 27km West of central Sydney.

It is also the name of an immigration detention centre built on the traditional lands of the Gandangara people.

The facility has been active since the early 90s and was a migrant hostel before that.

In early 2011 I visited Villawood for the first time with some friends.

I had no idea what to expect.

I walked through a metal detector and was checked for traces of drugs.

Everyone passes through a number of security doors.

No phones, cameras, money or anything sharp are allowed in the centre.

All watched by the camera's unblinking eye.

It's an environment of chain link fences...

And tall, sharp palisade rods topped with electric wire.

Even the trees were bound in corrugated iron and steel spikes.

I suppose to prevent someone from climbing them and jumping off.

The Villawood detention centre can hold up to 480 people.

Most are from Iran, Afghanistan, Sri Lanka, Myanmar and other repressive or war-affected places.

Most detainees are male, though the centre contains a block that houses 40-50 women, and a residential area for families.

The bulk have come to Australia from Indonesia by boat.

serco

'PEOPLE ARE OUR BUSINESS'

The centre is managed by Serco, a multinational corporation that also runs prisons in the UK.

6

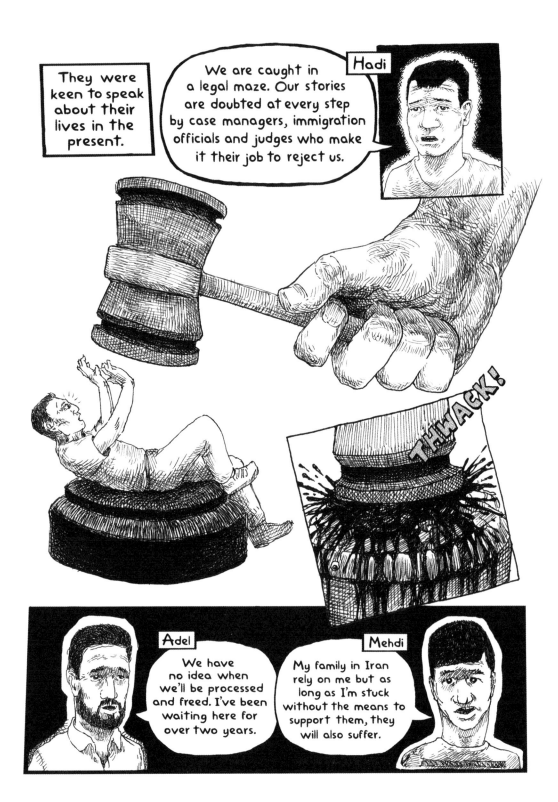

8

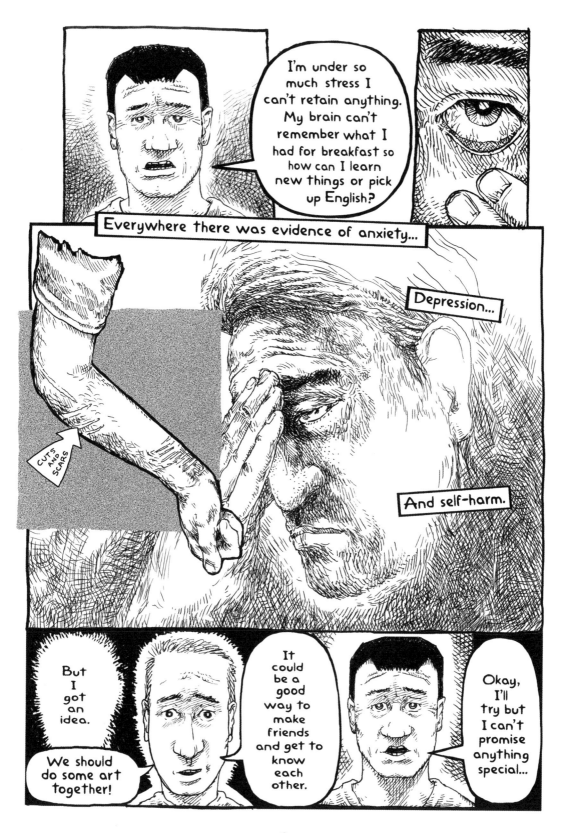

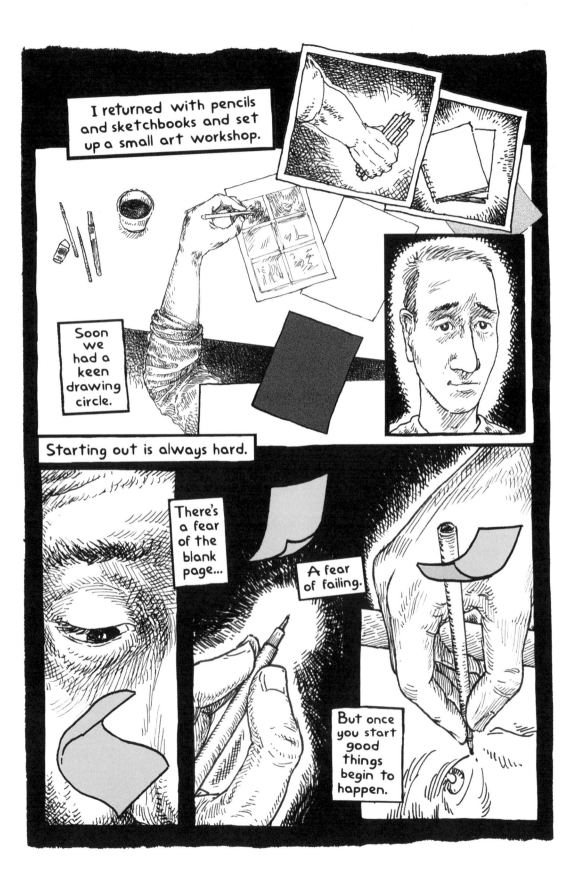

An average day in Villawood begins slow.

People stay up all night talking to their families back home.

Many sleep in till the early afternoon.

3:10 pm

Hi! Good morning! How are you?

It's a mundane everyday greeting...

Though hard to answer if you're going through hell.

Still alive.

11

So we ate, drew and jabbered about everything from politics to sport.

Fish curry needs turmeric...

I miss eating pakoras.

Did you see the cricket last night?

Do newsreaders wear ties?

They often don't wear pants.

Such conversations were often profound.

So why don't you like superhero movies?

How many of the drongos who love those movies will read the comics, heh?

NONE!

It was as much about making friends as making art.

Kids are always fun to muck around with.

And when language fails...

There's the eyebrow game!

Sri Lankan refugees made images about the war of 2009 and the subsequent persecution they experienced under the Rajapaksa government.

'Execution' by K. Waran

Hazara Afghans drew blood-curdling images of the Taliban.

'Death' by Bashir

A Rohingya Muslim man from Myanmar depicted the terrible trauma inflicted on his community.

'Burmese Golf' and 'Prison' by Mohammad.

It was enough to sate my curiosity about refugees...

And it motivated me to draw this comic - to explore these issues in more depth.

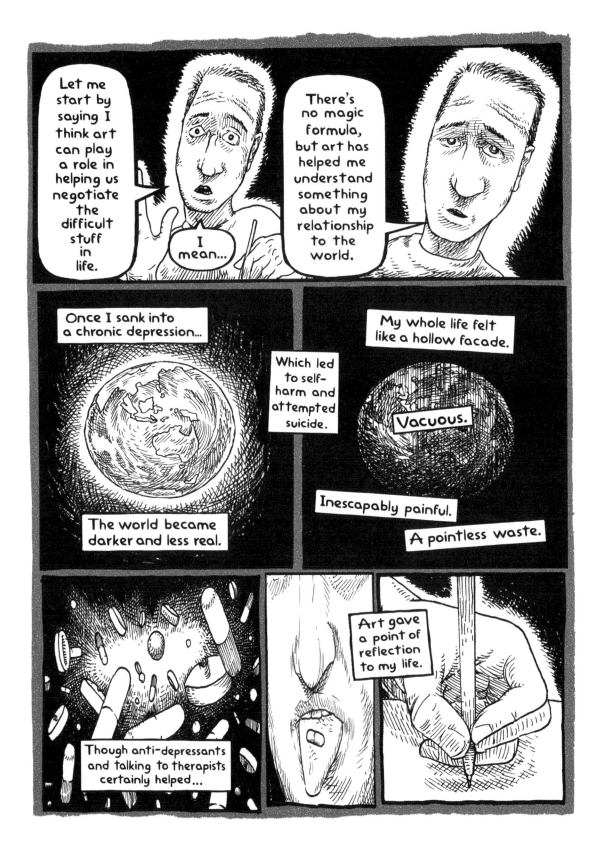

17

Mary Shelley's Frankenstein really got to me.

Yes the monster is capable of evil...

But what it really needs is love and companionship.

In its words:

'Everywhere I see bliss, from which I alone am irrevocably excluded. I was benevolent and good—misery made me a fiend.'

For me the novel's true message is that social exclusion can have terrible consequences and is worse than anything the monster could dream up.

And I too sometimes feel judged and isolated by the bulk of humanity.

I also crave love.

Ugghh...

19

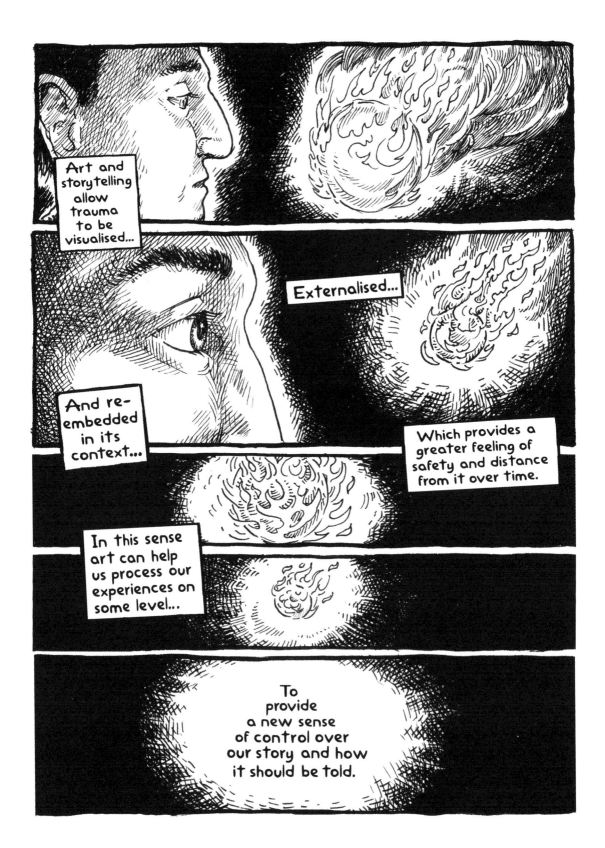

Art and storytelling allow trauma to be visualised...

Externalised...

And re-embedded in its context...

Which provides a greater feeling of safety and distance from it over time.

In this sense art can help us process our experiences on some level...

To provide a new sense of control over our story and how it should be told.

27

He drew poignant comics about life in detention.

I said goodbye to my family. My mum was crying.

I know that asylum seekers are normally released on a Tuesday or a Wednesday.

Every moment I pray that an officer will knock on my door and tell me that I'll be released today.

Sir, I want to write about my life.

I want people to know about the things I've been through.

A visitor asked me why I 'jumped the queue' the other day.

I described my idea of making this graphic novel and he wants to be a part of it.

(Like most people in this comic we changed his name for reasons of privacy.)

His story became our collaboration.

28

# HAIDER'S JOURNEY EXILE

I was born and raised in a village called Sharistan, in Toghai Afghanistan. My family belongs to the Hazara ethnic minority and being Shia Muslim we are also a religious minority.

The Taliban would attack our village because we are heretics in their eyes.

My brother was killed when he was 18 years old.

A year later my father was murdered.

They would capture or kill young men from our village. When I was 8 I saw the corpses of about 50 people who had been slaughtered.

My mum decided to leave Afghanistan and find somewhere safe.

When I was 13 I worked as a child labourer and farmhand to raise money for our survival. We lived in Iran illegally, without proper documents, which is the situation of many Afghans.

There are an estimated 3 million Afghan refugees living in Iran. They are given few work rights and are not allowed to become citizens.

We were discriminated against by everyone.

STOP!

At the age of 14 I was captured by the authorities and put in a deportation centre.

It was a large concrete structure with dirty walls.

Afghans had to pay for their own deportation.

If they didn't have enough money, they would be made to stay until someone paid for them.

There were about 40 or 50 people crammed into a single room.

They didn't care if we were going to be killed upon our return.

The authorities just wanted to get rid of us.

A bus took me and some other Afghans to Urmia, which is close to the Turkish border.

We were dropped off at a path which went into the mountains.

I came across more than 30 Afghans who were on the same journey.

The trek lasted 24 hours with only some dates, dried fruit and nuts to sustain us.

At last we arrived in a village in Turkey.

We were packed into a small truck and driven for 36 hours to Istanbul.

It was so cramped that you could only sit down holding your knees.

Once we arrived, an agent organised our transport to Greece.

We left Turkey at midnight on an inflatable raft and arrived on Lesbos about 11 hours later.

38

Some people lie on the wheel axle beneath the truck. This is the most dangerous place to hide because if the truck is empty and the driver decides to lift the wheels then the axle comes up and you can get crushed.

CRUNCH!

I climbed behind the wind deflector which goes over the driver's cabin.

It's a silly place to hide because it's easy to be seen from outside the truck.

But it worked.

Inside the ship I left my spot and found somewhere to sleep.

I knew the trip might take 40 hours.

Eventually I moved back to my original hiding place.

We left the ship and I jumped off the truck at some lights.

I washed at the first tap I could find.

I was told people would know I was a refugee if I looked dirty.

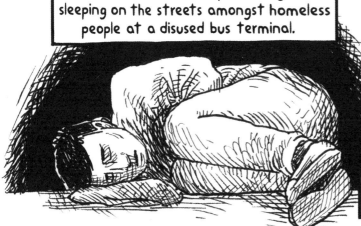

I was lost in Rome. I spent 2 nights sleeping on the streets amongst homeless people at a disused bus terminal.

Local church people came with food and blankets.

41

Paris was the worst.

Near Gare de l'Est I slept under a bridge by a river for 2 nights.

It was crowded with refugees.

Luckily someone let me share the tent his friend had just left.

It was so cold.

There were quite a few journalists doing stories about refugees though hardly anyone spoke with them.

I mean they are nice enough people...

But their stories don't change anything.

I was happy to get out of there.

Onward to Calais, to 'the jungle'.

That was the camp near the port, where you could find a truck.

When you get on one you don't know where it's going...

I just hoped mine was for England and not Belgium or Spain. The port in Greece did not have scanners whereas Calais did.

They use a laser to detect carbon dioxide from a person's breath inside the truck...

So people put plastic bags on their heads to avoid getting caught.

Again I hid above the driver, to avoid that.

I was very cold in that spot and felt relieved when we entered the ship.

I soon fell asleep.

Then I heard the wheel chains being released.

The truck was moving.

After a time I stuck my head out to have a look.

London 85

At some lights I jumped off the lorry and stood at the side of the highway. I was soon picked up by the police.

I told them everything.

I told them my mum had sent me to find somewhere safe. I was only fifteen at the time.

46

49

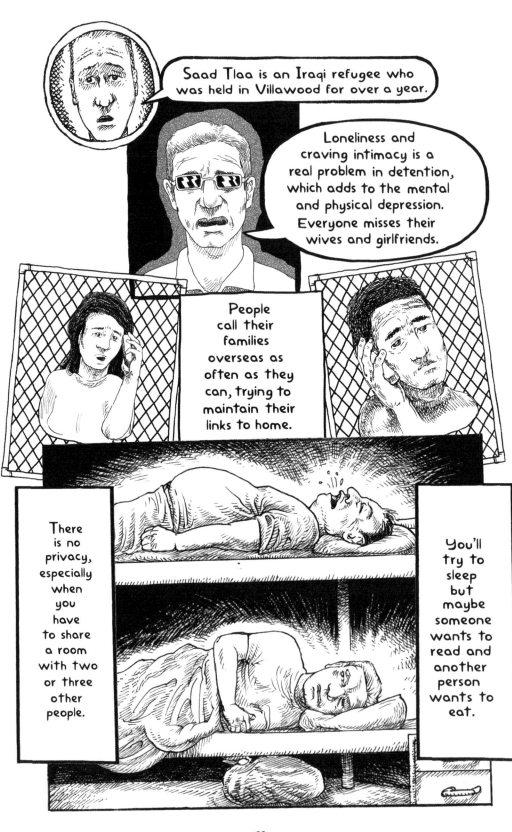

50

Young people would do their own thing. Some would try to court a woman in the centre and in some cases men would find intimacy with each other.

To sleep soundly I would be as active as possible and tire myself out during the day.

Then I would experience relief in my sleep!

The wet dreams occurred naturally.

Many would masturbate but the isolation is hard to get over.

Craving intimacy makes everything worse.

I knew a refugee from Algeria who was gay and we became friends. He tried to hide his sexuality from the other detainees, even though it was the basis of his refugee claim.

I think he was afraid of being physically or verbally abused in the centre.

He pretended to have a wife and would show people her photo but I knew he had found it on the internet.

His claim for protection was eventually accepted though it was hard for him to prove.

There was no way he could return to his country.

57

Marissa Ram, a human rights lawyer, confirmed this.

As an intern with the NSW Council for Civil Liberties I assisted asylum seekers who needed up-to-date country information about the places they were from, to support their refugee claims.

I saw that a number of human rights websites were blocked inside the centre. This impeded the legal process— by barring the information that would help refugees prove their case.

The computers are located in a common, recreational area where I try to avoid men, especially new people who I don't know.

You can't trust everyone and sometimes people have been inappropriate and rude to me.

It happens so often you get used to it and I forget that it's not even normal.

There are hundreds of stories like this...

They are the daily deprivations and abuses that result in a mass of depression and mental illness.

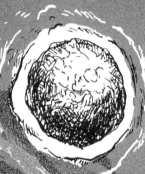

As most refugees see it: the system doesn't work...

And nor is it designed to.

They are in detention to be punished...

Not processed.

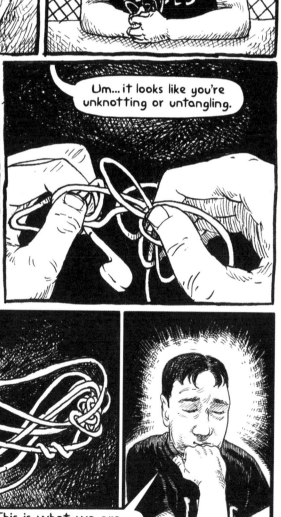

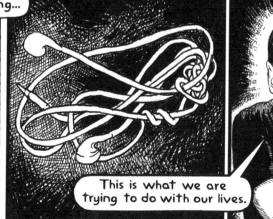

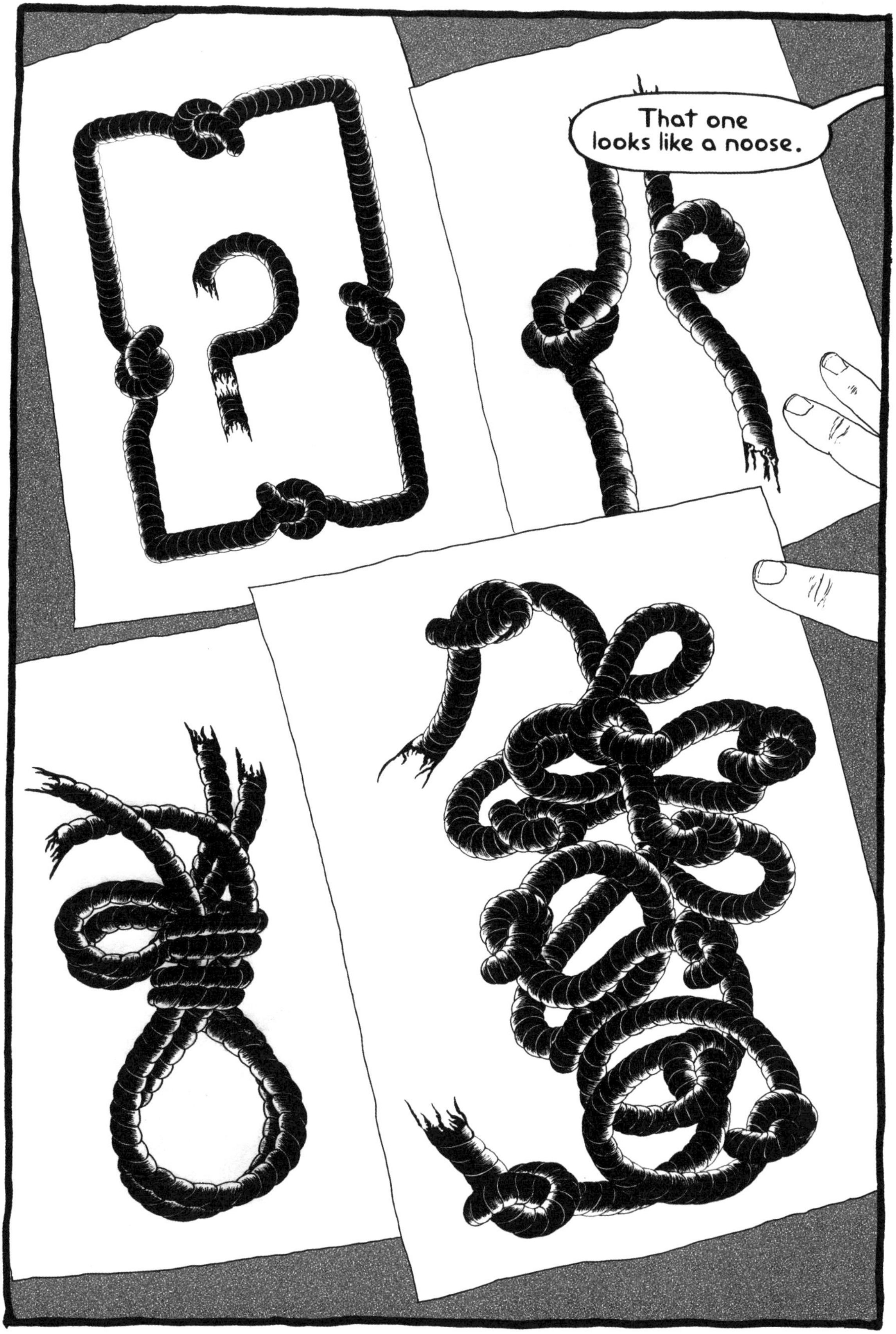
That one looks like a noose.

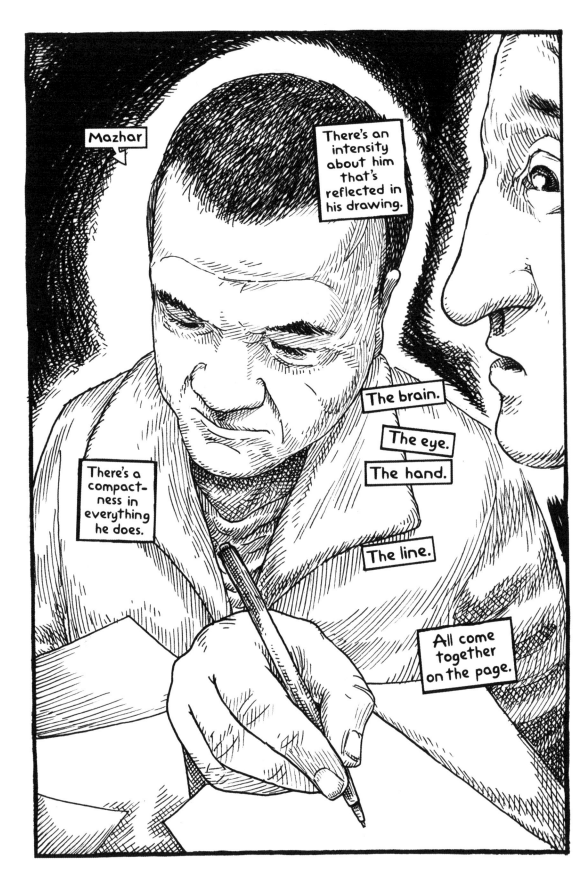

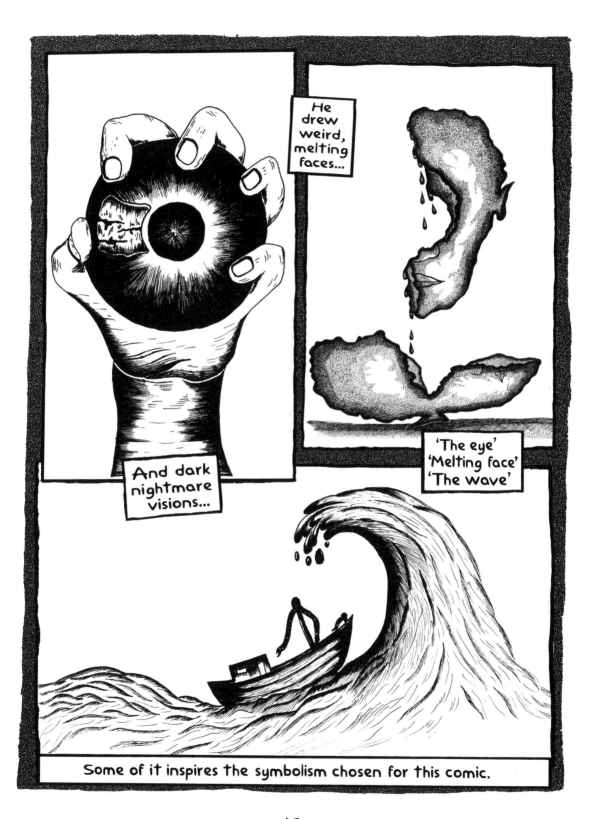

He drew weird, melting faces...

And dark nightmare visions...

'The eye'
'Melting face'
'The wave'

Some of it inspires the symbolism chosen for this comic.

When we left Indonesia it was pitch black and we couldn't even see what type of boat we were getting onto.

For the first few days of the journey we hid underneath the deck at all times.

This was to avoid being detected by Indonesian police or by the fishermen who tip them off for cash.

We met the captain at the start of our trip but in a few days he and the crew had disappeared.

They knew they would be punished in Australian custody.

Luckily some Sri Lankans who knew how to sail took charge of the boat and steered us towards Australia.

There were 55 people on board and most had never experienced the ocean before.

Most lost their energy and just lay around.

Everyone was burned.

One guy lost all the skin on his arm. It took at least a month for him to recover.

All I could think was I'm never going to see my mum again.

I'm going to die...

Here in the ocean.

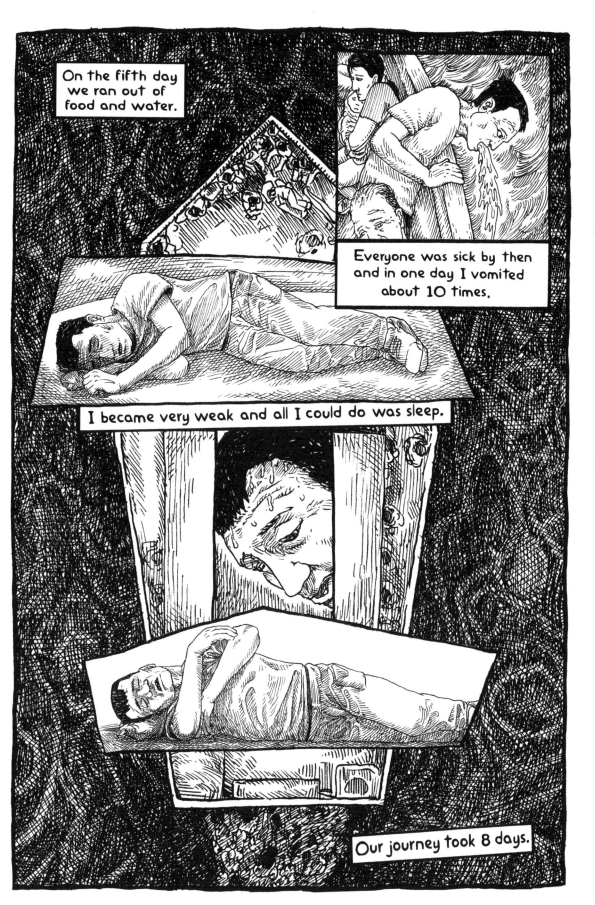

78

# HAIDER'S JOURNEY LIMBO

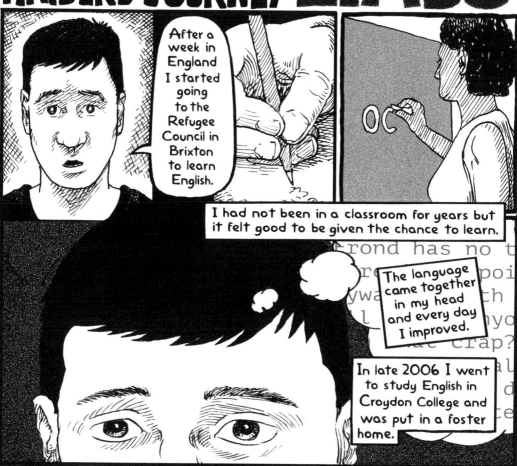

After a week in England I started going to the Refugee Council in Brixton to learn English.

I had not been in a classroom for years but it felt good to be given the chance to learn.

The language came together in my head and every day I improved.

In late 2006 I went to study English in Croydon College and was put in a foster home.

My carer was an English guy and it was just me and him living in the house.

I really enjoyed that time and he became like family to me.

When I was 16 I found a job and started working.

In a year I saved enough money to buy a car and get my driver's licence.

I was happy.

I was going out with friends on picnics, learning to kickbox and watching Bruce Lee movies.

As a child in Iran I would see kids going to school and I envied them so much.

I wanted to learn what they were learning.

I could fulfil that dream in England.

I would sometimes get emotional when I saw myself in the mirror wearing my uniform.

I made lots of friends amongst other refugees, including Ahmad Ali Jafari.

Ahmad also studied English and cooked the most delicious pizza, which he learned from working at a fast-food shop.

There's an unspoken look that passes between Hazara people.

Young or old, it's almost like you know them and know their story, even before you've met them...

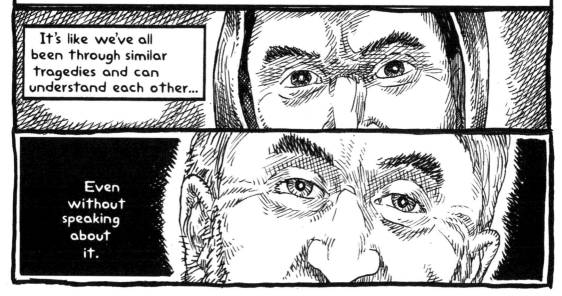

It's like we've all been through similar tragedies and can understand each other...

Even without speaking about it.

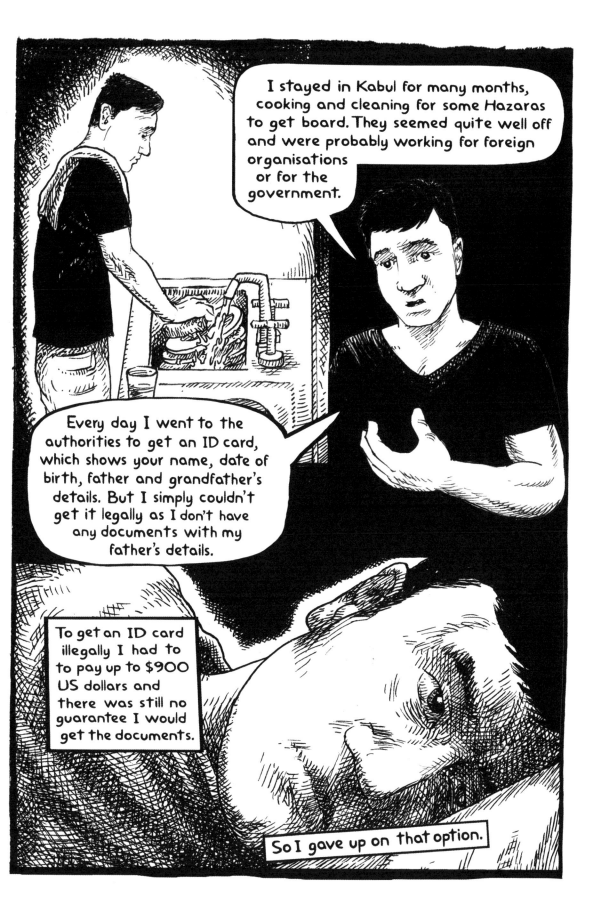

89

This began in the early 90s, when the Labor government did something no other country had tried.

It connected the refugee and humanitarian programs.

A cabinet document of June 1990 said:

Each applicant who is granted asylum in Australia displaces an applicant for humanitarian consideration overseas.

The idea of boat arrivals 'displacing' other refugees established the image of them as selfish 'queue jumpers' who manipulate Australia's generosity.

MINE!

CITIZENSHIP

In May 1992 Immigration Minister Gerry Hand introduced the policy of mandatory detention.

The Government is determined that a clear signal be sent that migration to Australia may not be achieved by simply arriving in this country and expecting to be allowed into the community.

Which unfortunately was how refugees and a large number of migrants have always come.

To increase the deterrence...

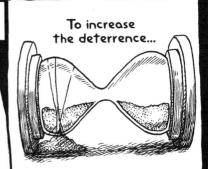

Any time limit on mandatory detention was removed in 1994, making Australia one of the only countries where refugees can be detained indefinitely.

95

Family reunions were not allowed under temporary visas nor were refugees allowed to travel outside of Australia.

This prompted hundreds of women and children to also come by boat - to be reunited with their husbands and fathers.

In October 2001 the SIEV X* sank between Indonesia and Christmas Island.

An estimated 146 children, 142 women and 65 men drowned.

Most were from Afghanistan and Iraq.

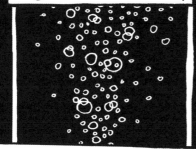

45 people were rescued after clinging to debris, and the corpses of those who had drowned, for over 20 hours.

Ruddock remained obstinate.

We have no obligation to give them rights and entitlements which become an incentive.

*'SIEV', meaning 'Suspected Illegal Entry Vessel', was the official acronym for a refugee boat at sea.

In December 2010 a boat carrying 90 asylum seekers smashed against the rocks of Christmas Island.

48 people were killed in the incident, which was beamed into living rooms across Australia, causing widespread shock.

Following the disaster both major political parties adjusted their narrative.

'Tough' policies of deterrence were necessary – not only to stop 'queue jumpers'...

'terrorists'...

'economic migrants'...

or people smugglers, who Prime Minister Kevin Rudd called:

Scum of the earth!

NO. Tough policies prevent drownings at sea.

This is about saving lives!

To show how much we care!

But are such policies legal?

102

The United Nations' 1951 Refugee Convention was drafted in response to the displacement of millions of people during the Second World War.

It defined a refugee as someone who cannot return to their country due to a 'well founded fear of being persecuted' for belonging to a particular race, religion, nationality, or social or political group.

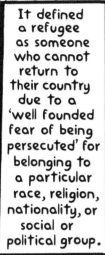

The Convention included the principle of non-refoulement, meaning refugees should not be sent back to a place of persecution.

They should not be punished for entering a country without proper documents or papers.

Nor should they be punished for <u>how</u> they enter a country.

Australia acceded to the principles of the Convention in 1954 and to the Protocol relating to the Status of Refugees in 1973.

Yet boat arrivals face a hard time the moment they are brought into custody.

Hadi

Having arrived at Christmas Island I was interviewed immediately. They asked about my identity and family history.

They asked why I left my country and other things, but we were all sick and tired so we didn't get to explain much.

A letter penned by doctors on Christmas Island in 2013 points out that in such interviews:

'Asylum seekers are examined while exhausted, dehydrated and filthy, their clothing soiled with urine and faeces.'

The problem is this interview is used by the department to try and catch the person out.

If a person forgets something later, or adds details to a memory, they'll say they are fabricating their story.

But personal histories cannot always be narrated concisely.

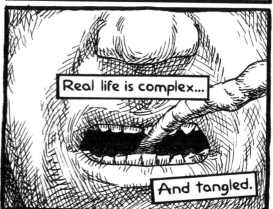

Real life is complex...

And tangled.

An official will ask why they did or didn't say something in order to test their 'credibility'.

This exploits the difficulty refugees face in telling their stories.

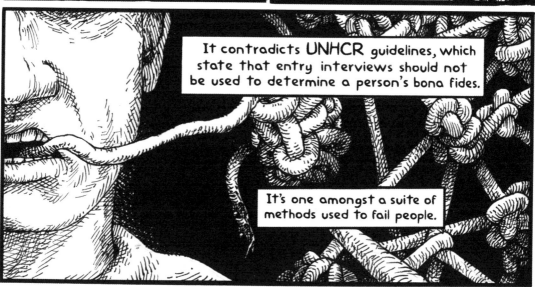

It contradicts UNHCR guidelines, which state that entry interviews should not be used to determine a person's bona fides.

It's one amongst a suite of methods used to fail people.

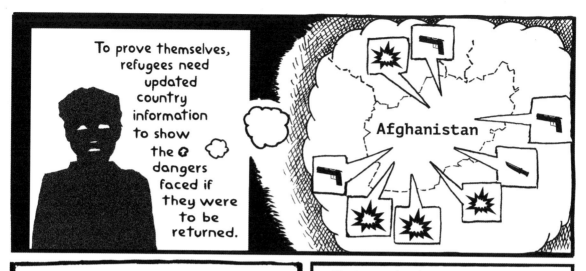

To prove themselves, refugees need updated country information to show the dangers faced if they were to be returned.

Afghanistan

To stump them government officials have used faulty data to deny people's protection claims.

In 2012 Steve Karas of the Refugee Review Tribunal was found by a Federal Court to have cut and pasted the same information into numerous reports justifying the rejection of Afghan asylum seekers instead of responding to the particulars of their case.

The first Afghan to be involuntarily deported in 2014 was Zainullah Naseri.

He was captured and tortured by the Taliban upon his return.

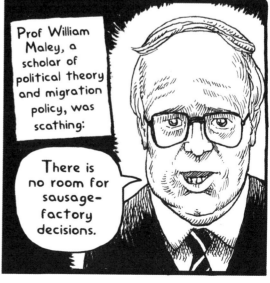

Prof William Maley, a scholar of political theory and migration policy, was scathing:

There is no room for sausage-factory decisions.

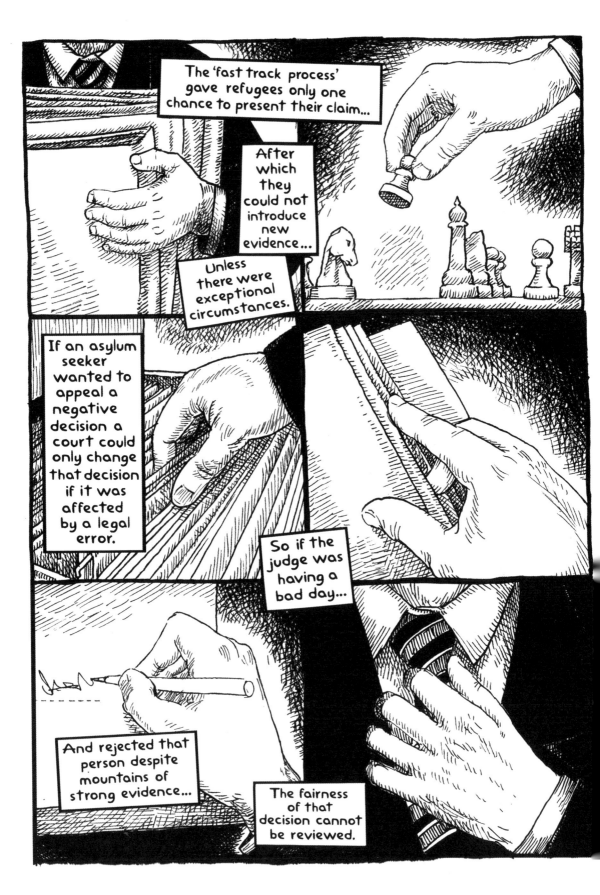

That same year the government imposed temporary visas on boat arrivals – blocking their chances of gaining permanent protection.

It also announced that any asylum seekers who came by boat would be denied legal support.

Many went into debt just to pay for legal representation or borrowed money from friends.

Children born to refugees in detention were to be considered 'transitory persons' and 'unauthorised maritime arrivals'.

Like their parents they were subjected to offshore processing...

And denied permanent protection.

For refugees living in the community, the government imposed a:

# CODE OF BEHAVIOUR

It warned against acts that are:

'Inconsiderate, disrespectful or threaten the peaceful enjoyment of other members of the community'.

This applied to such trivialities as:

'spitting'

and...

'swearing in public'.

CITIZEN

REFUGEE

Any breach of the code or incident involving the police meant a person was taken immediately to a detention centre.

What's going on?

F#@$!

F#@$!!

Hello is that the police?... There's someone disrespecting the peaceful enjoyment of the community!

You'll have to come with us.

This made refugees afraid to go to the police even if a crime was committed against them.

It made women experiencing domestic violence reluctant to report their husbands, knowing it would endanger their refugee process.

There is no official count of border-related deaths in Australia though a university study puts the number at well over 2000 people between the years 2000 to 2020.

Of those who entered an immigration detention facility, 23% were held for over 2 years.

By early 2018 the average time in detention for asylum seekers had reached 826 days.

Some had been detained for up to 10 years.

115

Aarrggh...

Well I'm not actually 'friends' with them as such...

I mean, I just got to know them through the workshop, you know?

So yeah... it's not like I knew them before as friends or anything.

Ok... Let me check on that with my manager and I'll get back to you.

A week or so later she called back...

Hi. So I've spoken to my manager and the answer is yes you can resume the art classes.

Umm...ok. Great.

A few months later some friends and I held an exhibition of artworks in collaboration with refugees.

'Freedom' by Ali Rahimi

People who were locked up for years seized the opportunity to express their frustration.

'Prison' by Mohammad

**Then we heard from the Department of Immigration:**

Dear Mr Ahmed,

This letter is to confirm that due to a confidentiality breach regarding artwork, you are no longer permitted to visit the Villawood Detention Centre.

**This included blocking our website on computers within the centre.**

### Access Denied

The link you are accessing has been blocked by the Barracuda Web Filter because it contains content belonging to the category of: Suspicious

If you believe this is an error or need to access this link please contact your administrator.

   URL: http://www.therefugeeartproject.com

   Login

   You may be able to gain access by authenticating with different credentials

This is an actual screengrab taken from a computer inside Villawood in 2012.

**Not that it mattered so much... I still went to Villawood as a casual visitor rather than as a volunteer.**

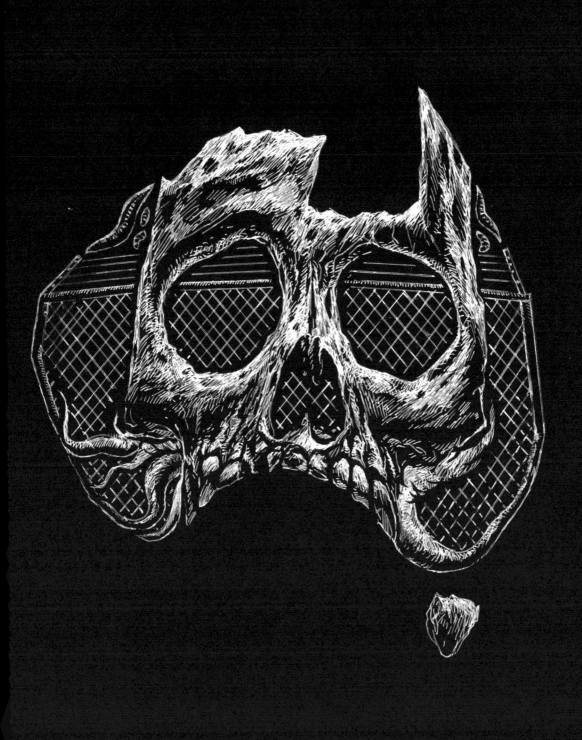

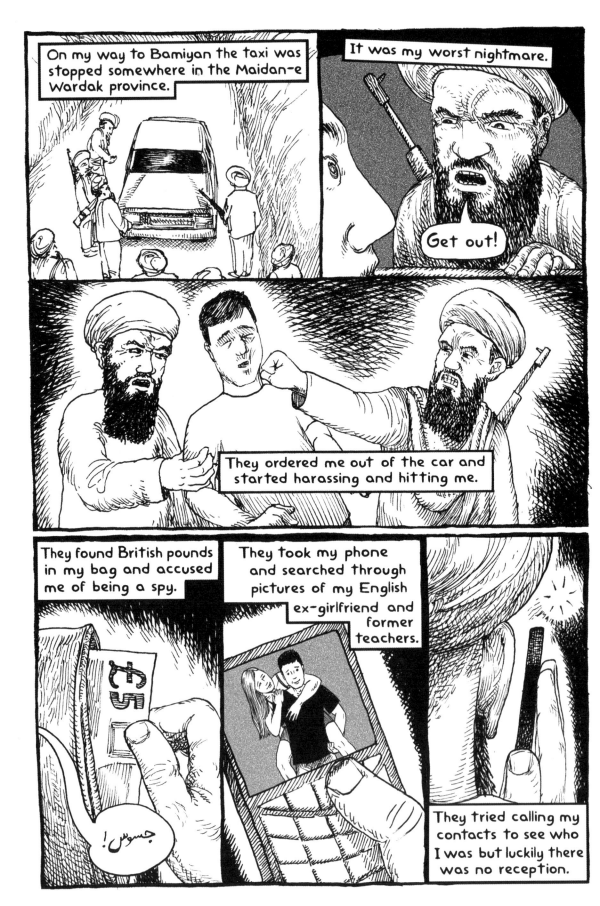

A window had been blocked over but I noticed some loose steel on the frame where the window used to be.

With that we started to dig under one of the walls.

I remembered how a dog will often dig in the soft soil under walls in old houses.

So we did the same.

It took about 3 hours to create a V-shape tunnel that I could slip through.

But Hussein was a bit fat so we dug for an extra half an hour.

We ran for an hour and a half, often stopping to hide if we thought there was a chance of being seen.

We arrived at a small dirt road and hid nearby.

We saw a van, though we didn't know if it was a Taliban vehicle.

When we saw there was only the driver...

We hailed it down.

The moment I landed at Sydney Airport I announced myself as a refugee. I drew this comic to show what happened that day.

# I AM NOT A CRIMINAL

I'm from Afghanistan. I came to Australia to apply for assylum.

At Sydney Airport I was interviewed by an immigration officer.

So why did you leave your country?

I fled because of the Taliban.

I'm afraid we have to put you in detention.

But I haven't done anything wrong!

I'm sorry you've failed immigration clearance.

4 months later

Why are they keeping me here? I'm not a criminal!

How much longer will I be here?

131

When I first entered Villawood I was scared.

I had no idea where they were taking me.

Then I saw an old face!

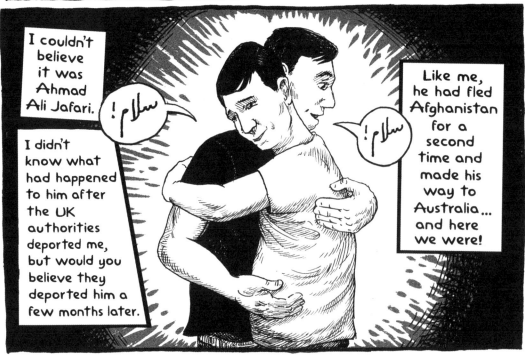

I couldn't believe it was Ahmad Ali Jafari.

I didn't know what had happened to him after the UK authorities deported me, but would you believe they deported him a few months later.

سلام!

سلام!

Like me, he had fled Afghanistan for a second time and made his way to Australia... and here we were!

# AHMAD

Ahmad Ali Jafari became a regular presence at our workshops.

Would you like tea or coffee?

A generous, warm-natured man, he prepared drinks for everyone in the room.

We joked about his trademark sleek, black hair.

SWOOSH!

Like so many refugees in detention, his artwork expressed the frustration of being indefinitely detained with no certainty of release.

Suddenly they put me in the Villawood detention centre.

133

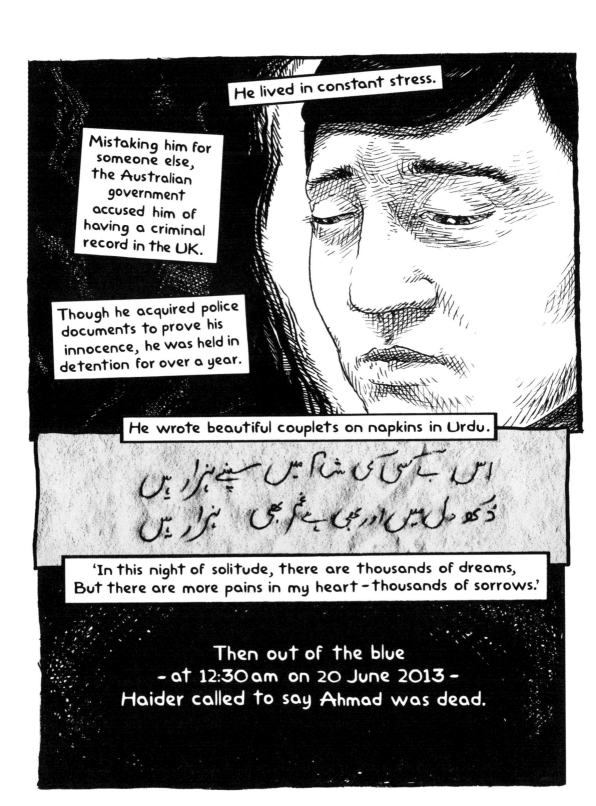

He lived in constant stress.

Mistaking him for someone else, the Australian government accused him of having a criminal record in the UK.

Though he acquired police documents to prove his innocence, he was held in detention for over a year.

He wrote beautiful couplets on napkins in Urdu.

اس بے کسی کی شام میں سینے ہزار ہیں

دکھ دل میں اور بھی ہے غم بھی ہزار ہیں

'In this night of solitude, there are thousands of dreams,
But there are more pains in my heart - thousands of sorrows.'

Then out of the blue
- at 12:30 am on 20 June 2013 -
Haider called to say Ahmad was dead.

I went to get Ahmad some water and as I re-entered the room I saw a Serco officer joking and laughing at him.

Haha! That's bullshit!

I think he thought Ahmad was making the whole thing up just so he could get his own room.

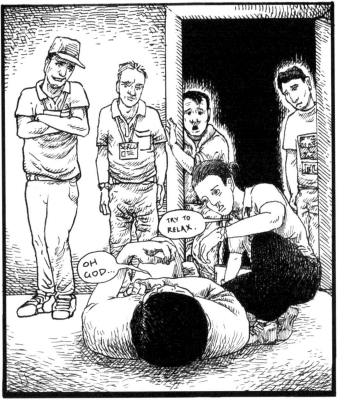

TRY TO RELAX.

OH GOD...

The nurse came and asked the supervisor to call an ambulance.

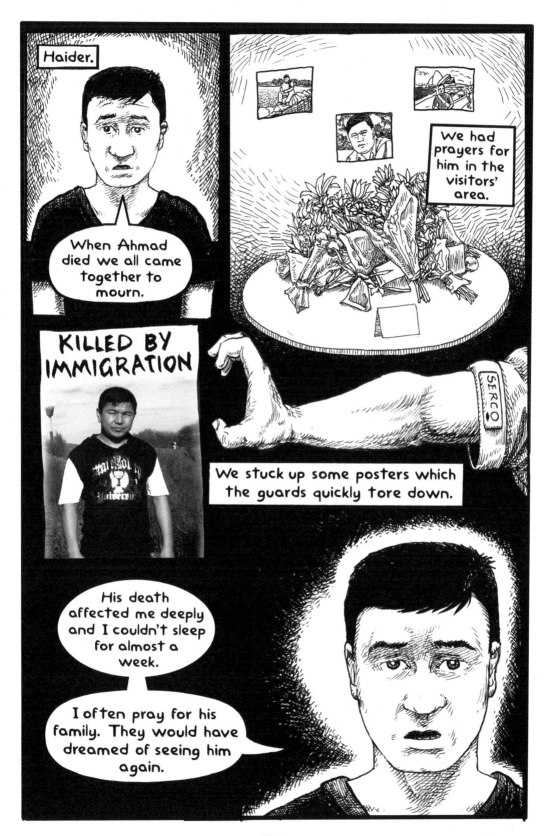

139

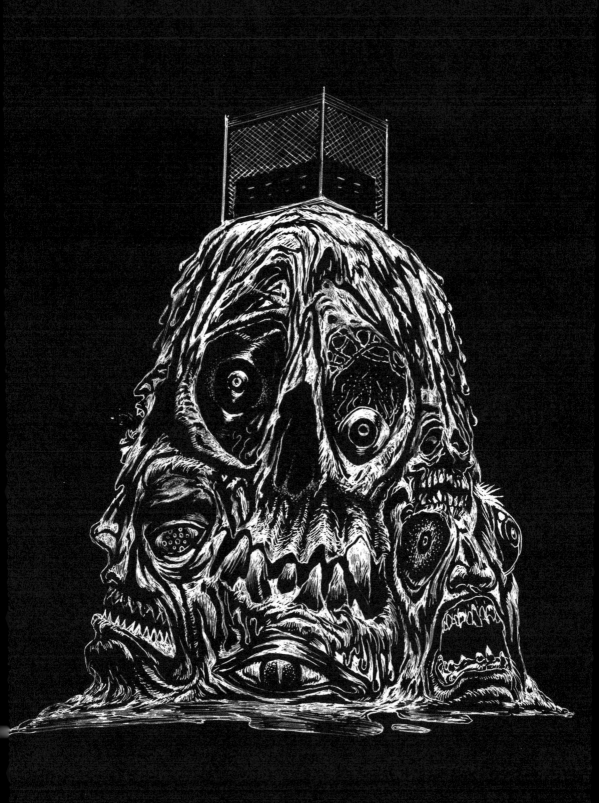

In August 2001 a Norwegian freighter Tampa rescued 422 asylum seekers whose ship was mired at sea.

We were proud to help them.

Seizing an opportunity to appear strong on border protection the Australian government ordered the vessel to stay out of its waters, which the captain ignored.

Realising some needed urgent medical attention, Captain Arne Rinnan steered the vessel towards Christmas Island.

This created a stand-off that would last for 9 days.

That boat will never land in our waters —NEVER!

The government sent heavily armed SAS troops to storm the vessel.

Prime Minister John Howard

Australia tried to persuade Indonesia and Norway to accept the people though both countries declined.

144

The asylum seekers were then taken to a makeshift camp in the tiny island nation of Nauru, which is not a signatory to the UN Refugee Convention.

This became known as the 'Pacific Solution', where people arriving by boat were sent to Australian-funded detention camps in Nauru and Manus Island in Papua New Guinea.

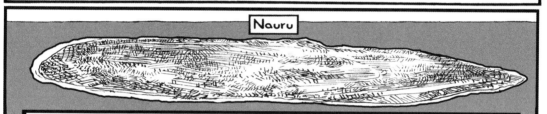

1637 people were detained in those facilities over 7 years, including 786 Afghans, 684 Iraqis and 88 Sri Lankans. Most were found to be refugees and were eventually resettled in Australia and other countries.

The 'Tampa-affair' as it became known won John Howard and the Australian Liberal Party the national election in 2001.

Nauru and Manus Island ran until 2008 but were re-opened by the Labor Party in 2012.

Australia's offshore camps are a legal black site for ensuring that asylum seekers have no access to judicial review under Australian law.

The political determination to keep them out of the country implicitly recognises this. As Labor Prime Minister Kevin Rudd put it in 2013:

From now on any asylum seeker who arrives by boat will have no chance of being settled in Australia.

Some of the buildings were run down World War II era structures.

I was placed in Oscar Compound, which held about 500 people.

In February 2014 frustration mounted after detainees were told they had no prospect of resettlement.

Protests within the centre soon broke into a riot, led by disaffected Iranians.

Local Manusians and people employed to look after the asylum seekers gathered outside the fence, armed with weapons, rocks, knives and machetes.

They broke in.

Detainees were beaten mercilessly.

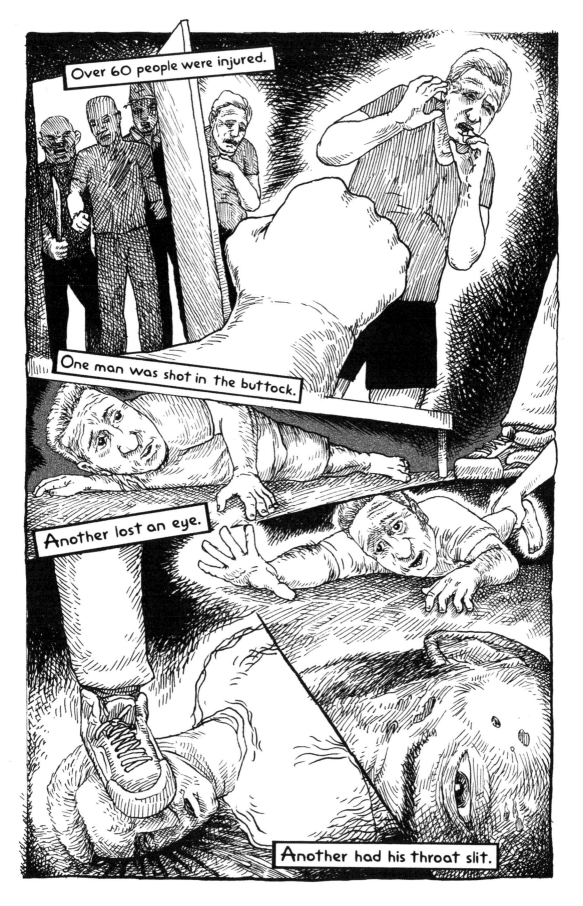

In March 2015, PNG's Supreme Court ruled that the detention of asylum seekers on Manus Island was 'illegal and in breach of the right to personal liberty' according to the PNG constitution.

The centre was opened, allowing some freedom of movement for refugees, though many were too afraid to go into local towns for fear of assault.

The same month the UN Human Rights Council condemned the Australian government for subjecting refugees in offshore detention centres to 'cruel, inhuman, and degrading treatment', in other words— torture.

WE ARE ASYLUM SEEKERS WE CALL FOR HELP PNG IS NOT SAFE

Australia absolved itself of responsibility, arguing that the fate of detainees was an issue for the Papua New Guinean and Nauruan governments.

The atmosphere on the islands remained volatile.

The Australians were responsible for that.

They told the local people we were all like terrorists who had done the wrong thing. They told the refugees the people of PNG were cannibals who would cut our throats if they could.

157

I acted as an interpreter and advocate for the most vulnerable asylum seekers on the island.

LGBTIQ people were intimidated and afraid of people inside and outside the camp.

They were harassed by everybody, including the security guards.

They were often bullied and forced to have sex with refugee guys who were not homosexual.

There was an incident in which a homosexual man was raped by other people in the shower rooms, in a block of toilets.

The people of Papua New Guinea are deeply hospitable.

And although Manusians were sympathetic towards the refugees they were unable to treat their dire physical and mental health needs.

While the centre brought some employment to Manus, there was no meaningful investment in local communities.

PNG authorities moved in and demolished the centre in October 2017.

Many refused to leave, fearing for their safety amongst the local community.

They occupied the site for many weeks.

Even after the power and water were shut off.

In November 2017 PNG forces bashed, dragged and forcibly relocated the remaining detainees to 'Transit Centres' (ie further limbo) in other parts of the island.

164

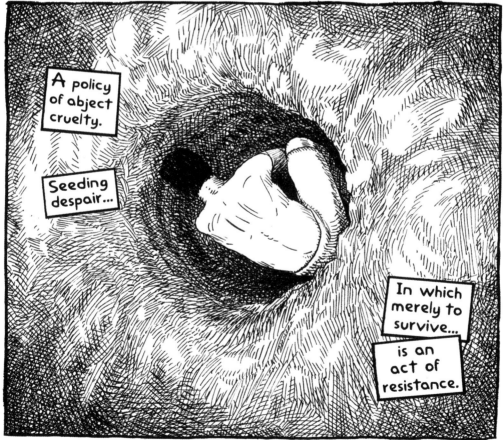

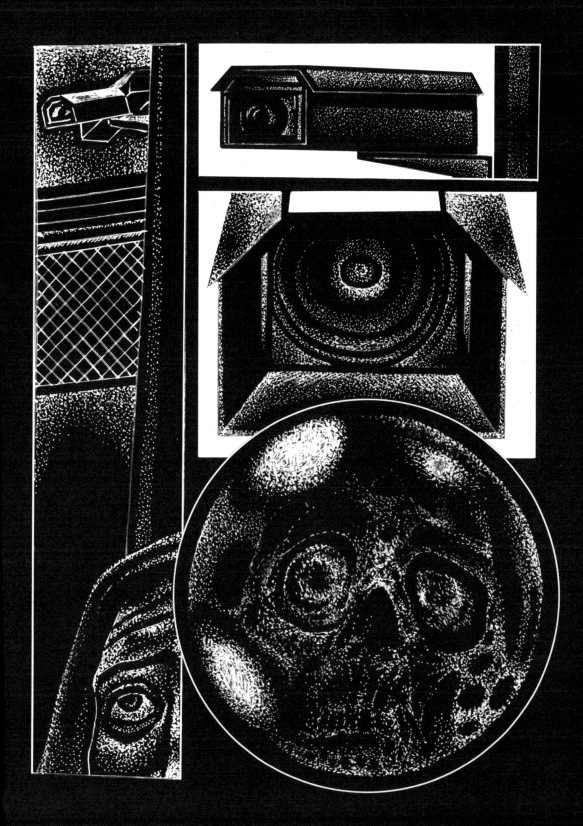

# STILL ALIVE...

There is no doubt that the mandatory and indefinite detention of asylum seekers and refugees erodes their mental and physical health.

Jonathan Phillips is a psychiatrist and former president of the Royal Australian and New Zealand College of Psychiatrists. He has treated numerous refugees in detention.

The effect of indefinite detention is quite profound.

The central issue is a process of chronic demoralisation, where a person's sense of self-esteem and purpose in life is eroded over a period of time.

The person probably has no prospect of overcoming that in the long term.

It's particularly hard for women and children.

A test case for this was the tiny island nation of Nauru, where over 800 asylum seekers, mostly families, were held for over 5 years.

Hundreds lived in humid tents which were overrun with mould and cockroaches.

In 2016 a cache of 2000 leaked documents revealed numerous allegations of abuse on Nauru.

They included allegations of sexual assault against women and threats of sexual assault.

7 sexual assaults against children.

Australia denied responsibility for their welfare which it palmed off to the Nauruan government.

FREEDOM

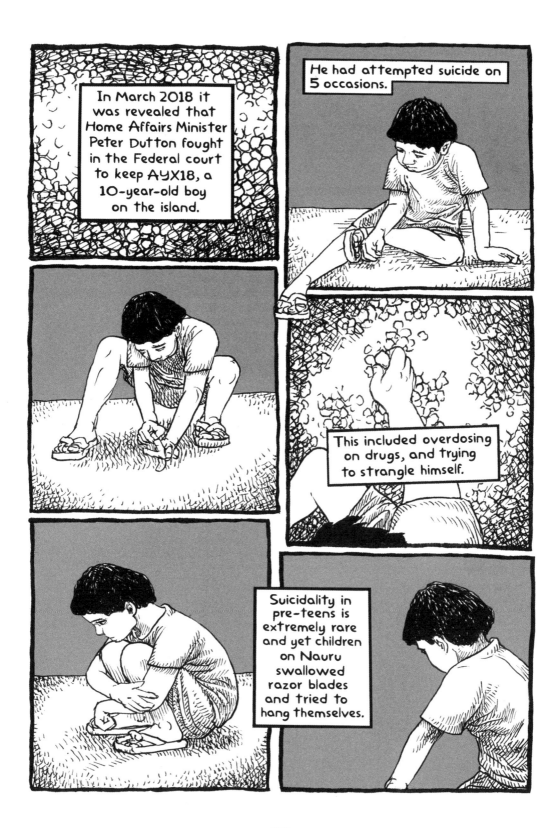

In March 2018 it was revealed that Home Affairs Minister Peter Dutton fought in the Federal court to keep AYX18, a 10-year-old boy on the island.

He had attempted suicide on 5 occasions.

This included overdosing on drugs, and trying to strangle himself.

Suicidality in pre-teens is extremely rare and yet children on Nauru swallowed razor blades and tried to hang themselves.

# ihms

IHMS (International Health and Medical Services) are contracted to provide health and psychological support for people in detention.

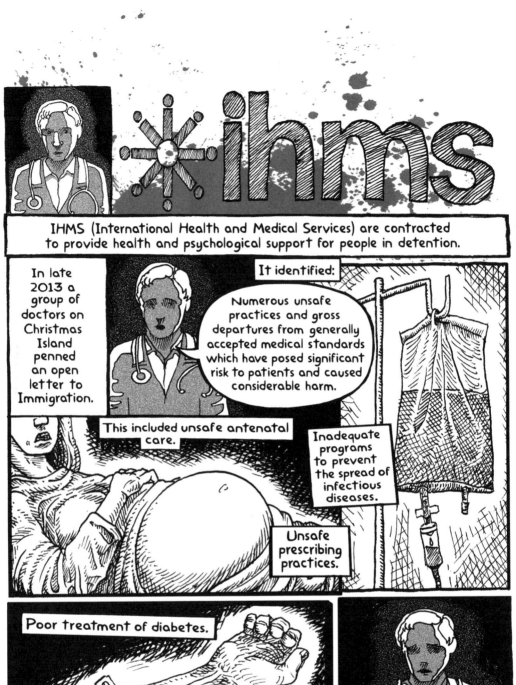

In late 2013 a group of doctors on Christmas Island penned an open letter to Immigration.

It identified:

Numerous unsafe practices and gross departures from generally accepted medical standards which have posed significant risk to patients and caused considerable harm.

This included unsafe antenatal care.

Inadequate programs to prevent the spread of infectious diseases.

Unsafe prescribing practices.

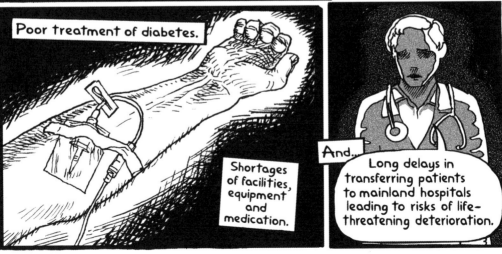

Poor treatment of diabetes.

Shortages of facilities, equipment and medication.

And...

Long delays in transferring patients to mainland hospitals leading to risks of life-threatening deterioration.

Such concerns became a reality in September 2014 when Hamid Khazaei, a 24-year-old Iranian asylum seeker, presented to the Manus clinic with an infected sore on his lower leg.

36 hours of intravenous antibiotics failed to reduce his fever.

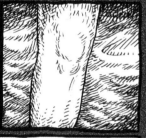

He developed an accelerated pulse, low blood pressure, vomiting, and could not walk to the toilet unaided.

A doctor ordered his urgent medical transfer, which went through 4 layers of bureaucracy.

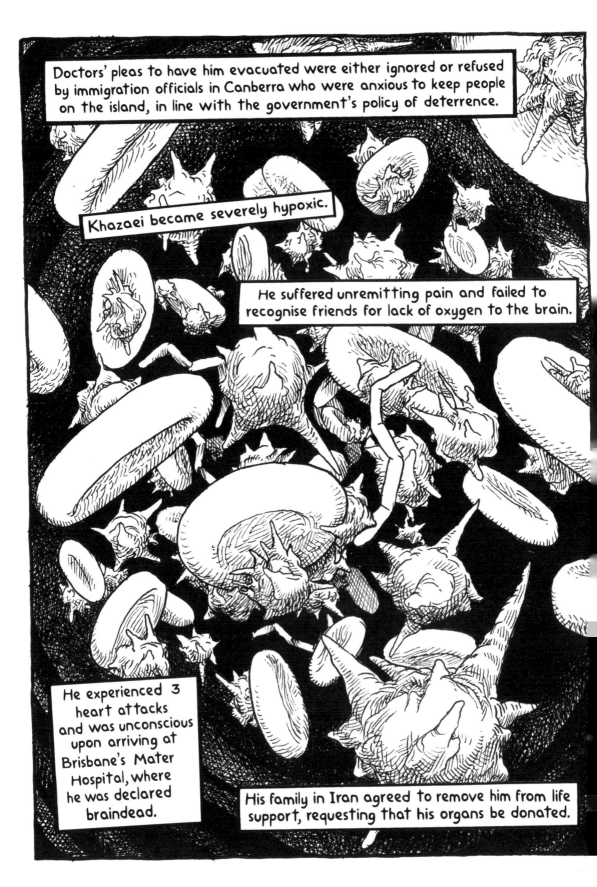

Doctors' pleas to have him evacuated were either ignored or refused by immigration officials in Canberra who were anxious to keep people on the island, in line with the government's policy of deterrence.

Khazaei became severely hypoxic.

He suffered unremitting pain and failed to recognise friends for lack of oxygen to the brain.

He experienced 3 heart attacks and was unconscious upon arriving at Brisbane's Mater Hospital, where he was declared braindead.

His family in Iran agreed to remove him from life support, requesting that his organs be donated.

175

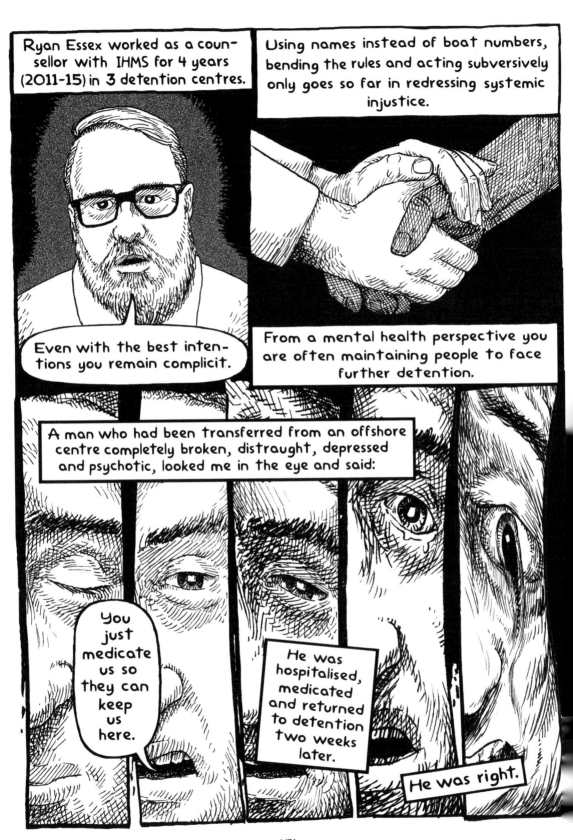

176

Dr Jonathan Phillips

When I was director of mental health in South Australia it became obvious to me that IHMS was not a health provider in the usual sense of the word where the focus is to provide best possible care to detainees with health problems.

The real master was the government. IHMS had to report to the government and therefore became skewed in its activities.

Munawar in Villawood spelled it out for me.

I've been getting worse every day but the psychologists don't help.

They make it seem as though we're normal because that's what Immigration wants to hear.

I don't want to see their shit psychologists anymore.

From a mental health perspective we are doing something which is barbaric, sadistic and contrary to international conventions.

In Villawood I became the 'art guy' who draws people.

Here's a drawing of a female guard, by Saeed.

And here's one he did of me, which is weird...

I'm a little self-conscious so it's strange,

to be interpreted by another person.

I don't know why it looks like I have an earring...

But I love this pic.

serco

178

Sometimes refugees are held up in a positive light.

It's true they have been award-winning...

Athletes

Surgeons

And comedians

They've shown incredible resilience to escape from persecution and survive their journeys.

They have so much to offer...

But these factors should never condition their acceptance.

People who have been through hell do not have to be angels.

They do not have to benefit anyone...

Most will be as ordinary...

Lazy...

Flawed...

And as unimpressive as you or I.

Me in the morning.

# HAIDER'S JOURNEY RELEASE

When they decided to release me from Villawood I was so excited.

Case manager

You will be transferred into the community though your claims are still proceeding.

Oh wow! I can't believe I'm getting out. Thank you so much!

Yeah well...

It's just more paperwork for me.

Villawood Immigration
...ntion Centre

SECURITY NOTICE

VIDEO SURVEILLANCE
IN USE ON
THESE PREMISES

RESTRICTED
AREA

NO
THOROUGHFARE

Hello sir?

I'm out!

Ah no way!

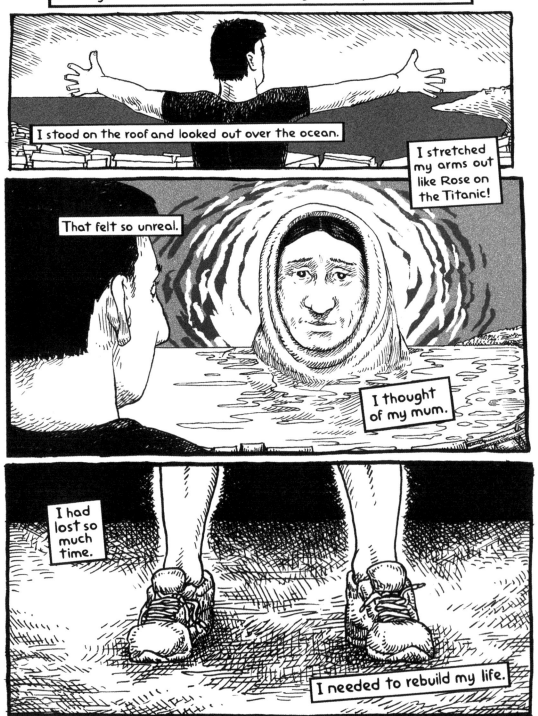

The day I left Villawood and went to my friend's place in Coogee...

I stood on the roof and looked out over the ocean.

I stretched my arms out like Rose on the Titanic!

That felt so unreal.

I thought of my mum.

I had lost so much time.

I needed to rebuild my life.

I found work in construction.

I joined a gym and got back into kickboxing.

And became a Coogee lifeguard on the weekends.

The other day I had my first official fight.

I thought here's a chance to finally show what I can do.

We were fighting under Muay Thai rules though I had trained in K-1, which combines different styles of fighting, including kickboxing and traditional boxing.

The fight started pretty evenly.

He tried to punch me early on but I'm good at evasion.

Then he started to clinch and hold whenever I got close.

In that position he could knee me quite easily cause he was taller.

It wasn't really connecting and it didn't hurt.

But he got cheap points for it.

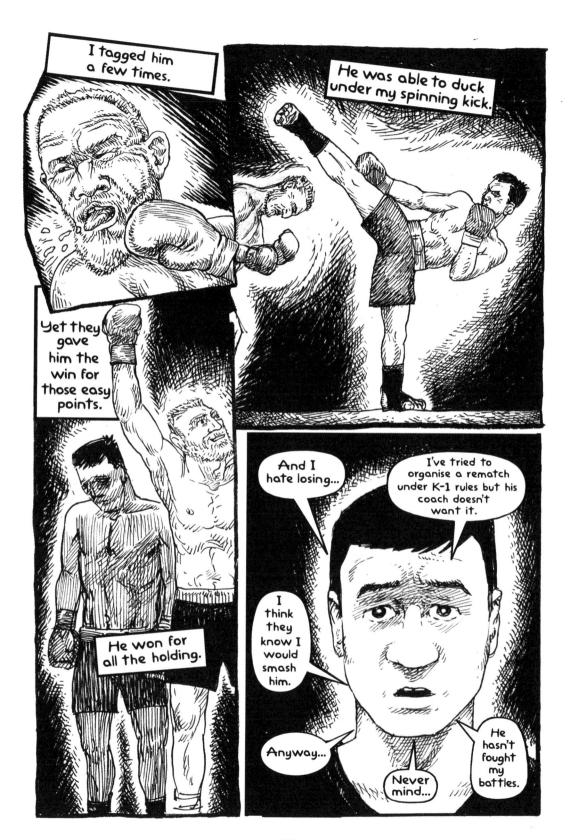

191

# POST-DETENTION DIMENSIONS

Post-detention, many struggle re-adjusting to life in the community.

I was locked up for 2 years.

Ali

The largest space was the visitor's and recreational areas, which weren't huge.

I remember New Year's Eve.

My friends and I saw fireworks in the sky and it was amazing. I thought one day we'll get out and see them.

My room had space for one bunk bed.

I slept on top but it was so cramped I had to be careful of the other person when I went to the toilet at night.

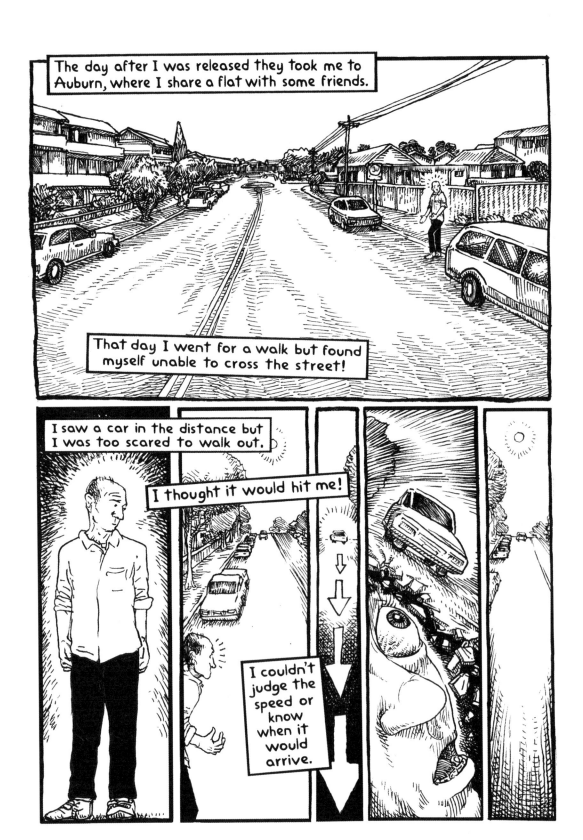

For the first week I didn't go further than **200** metres from our house.

I hadn't been outside in 2 years.

I was scared of people on the street.

I could not imagine how they saw me.

I felt different to everyone else...

So I watched to see if I was acting like them, and walking like they were walking.

Needless to say, it took some time.

One day in our studio...

Hey we need to get a coffee machine. I can't go without coffee.

Um ok... Let's have a look.

Ooh this one looks good! Someone's selling it at half price.

Let me pay something for this. In Villawood we...

Nah it's all good mate. We have some money to cover this.

Brother let me do this! I'm serious about...

But it's ok! We have the moulah so it's not an issue.

Listen...

In detention we didn't have this.

Imagine begging an officer for sugar just to make a drink.

Later...

Oh yeah!

That is damn good.

196

197

We began to host an art workshop for women of a refugee background.

I brought some cake.

How do you draw faces?

She looks like a ninja...

My son passed his exams.

That's where I met Elham.

She had just been released from detention a few months before.

Her drawings were so good.

As were the smells in that room.

Ghorma Sabzi is an Iranian dish made with lime, kidney beans, lamb and various herbs.

199

Elham's story I think captures some of the ambivalences and contradictions of what it means to feel caught between 2 places.

I came to Australia in 2012 with my mum and my sister, because we had a problem with Iran's government.

My dad had to stay behind.

I left for Australia hoping to study and make friends.

It was like a dream.

Under pressure to leave we had to trust people smugglers. We went through Bali and stayed in Jakarta for about 2 months. Our visa only lasted one month and we didn't know how to renew it. We were afraid to go shopping.

There were 115 people on our boat including a bunch of kids and a newborn baby.

It was August 2012.

Thankfully the sea was quiet.

At one point our engine died and the boat was leaking.

We were seen by an American yacht which waited with us until the Australian navy came. They gave us water bottles.

When the navy arrived I felt relieved.

I mean, at least we hadn't died at sea.

They brought us on the ship and burned the smuggler's boat.

It went up on the water like a box of matches.

It was hard to wash on Christmas Island. The bathroom was filthy and too small to get changed in.

Outside the shower block was a group of men who would stare at my legs.

None of the women felt safe.

One time I was in my room trying on a bra when I saw someone peering in through the window. I can't tell you how bad that was.

The officers would try and have relationships with women in the camp.

Hi.

They would say they were single and pretend to be available...

But when I got out I saw that some were married and had kids.

I spent time with my friend Maryam.

We would go to the fence and stare at the crabs.

203

# RESISTANCE

There are many ways in which refugees express their agency and resist the conditions of detention.

Some pore over the details of their case, researching the proof that may ensure their release.

Despite the odds many will master English while living in detention.

There's the continuation of familiar social, cultural and artistic practices.

Some will refuse to sign petty documents, such as good behaviour contracts.

If broken, the contract includes such punishments as cancelling visits and internet access.

Other types of resistence include foot-dragging.

Resisting deportation.

Speaking to the media.

DEFIANCE.

Hunger strikes and refusing to take medication.

Self-harm is an expression of abject despair but in detention it's sometimes more than that.

Because refugees are dehumanised...

Because they are reduced to the status of incarcerated bodies...

To harm themselves is to defy the system that locks them away.

In October 2015 the Afghan Hazara asylum seeker Khodayar Amini burnt himself to death in bushland near Dandenong, Victoria.

The day before his death he wrote:

"My crime was that I was a refugee.

They tortured me for 37 months and... treated me in the most cruel and inhumane way.

They violated my basic human right and took away my human dignity with their false and so called humane slogans.

I write this statement with my blood for those who call themselves human beings...

I ask you to stand up for the rights of refugees...

Humanity is not a slogan; every human being has the right to live."

# PROTEST

My name is Yusuf and I am a Hazara refugee from Afghanistan.

I had been in detention for one and half years.

I hadn't heard from my case officer in 4 months.

So in February 2012 I joined a rooftop protest in Villawood.

I couldn't take it anymore.

I wanted the Department of Immigration to speed up my case.

That was my only request.

The protest soon became a riot and all the refugees in Villawood were punished.

I was taken by police and held in Silverwater prison for the next 2 weeks.

In the end they did not charge me with anything but it was the worst time of my life.

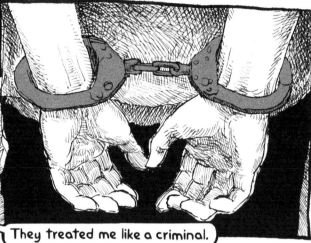

They treated me like a criminal.

Just because I came by boat...

To escape the Taliban.

YOU FUCKEN QUEUE JUMPER!

The prison guards abused me...

But I am a refugee.

I only came here to save my life and Australian politicians tried to destroy me.

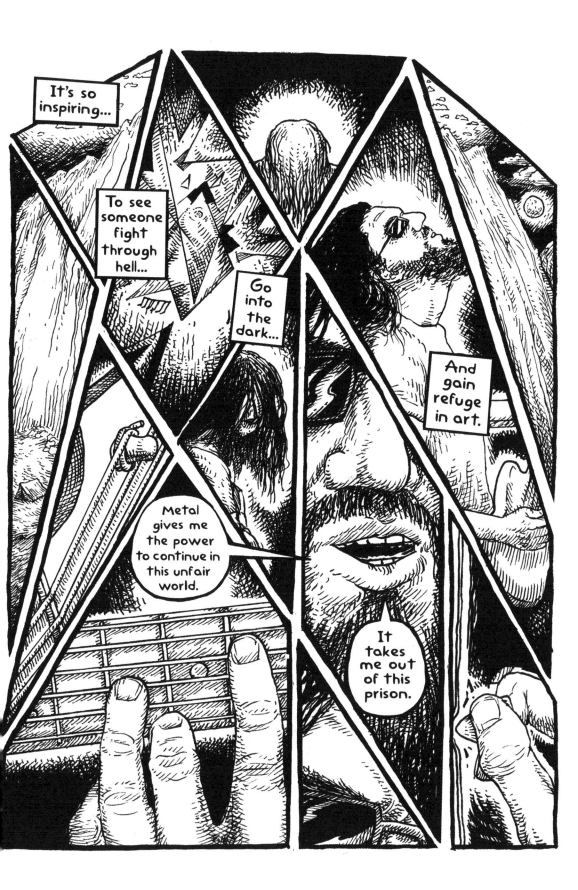

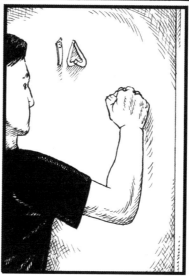

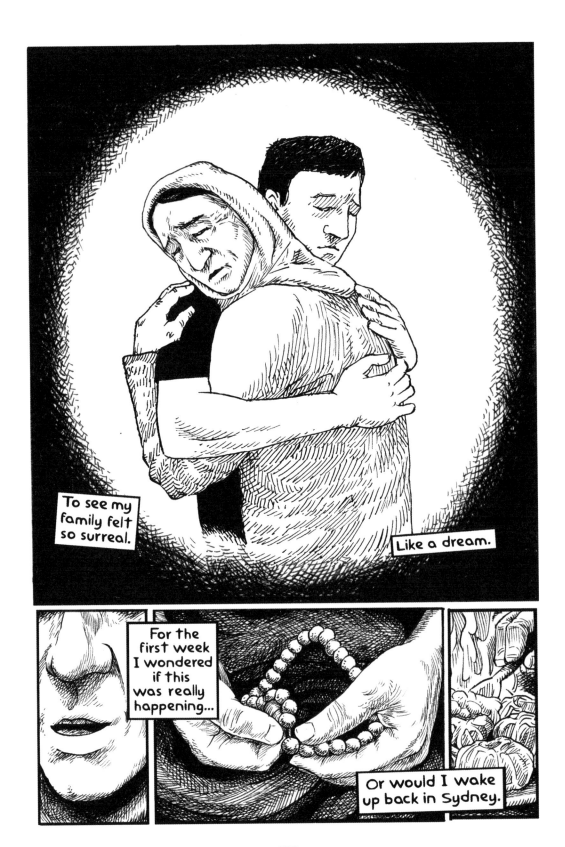

To see my family felt so surreal.

Like a dream.

For the first week I wondered if this was really happening...

Or would I wake up back in Sydney.

I showed the draft of this comic to Haider.

Here you go, mate. It's not perfect but I hope you like it.

Thanks... sir.

Ah you put in my kickboxing!

I'm glad you show me fighting someone who looks like Connor McGregor.

STILL ALIVE DRAFT #

That d$#k was so racist to Khabib!

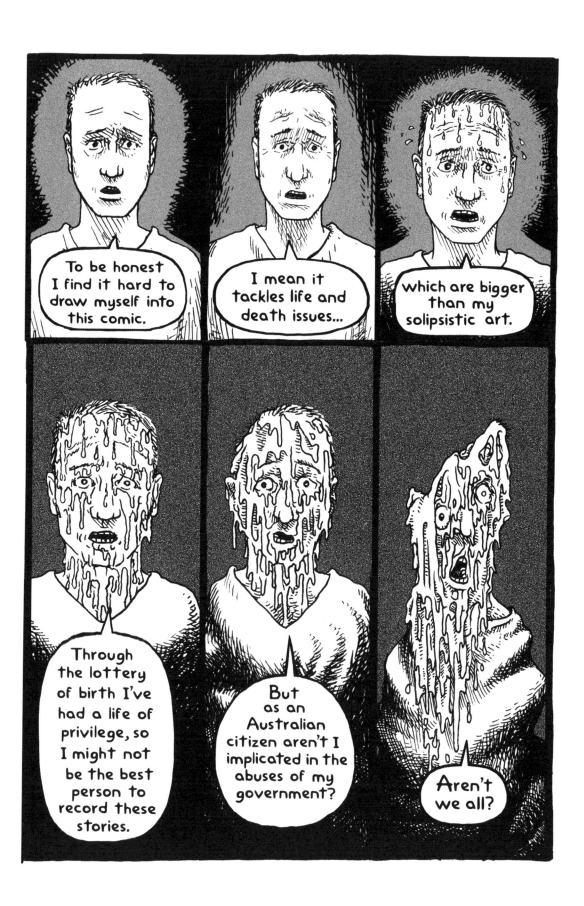

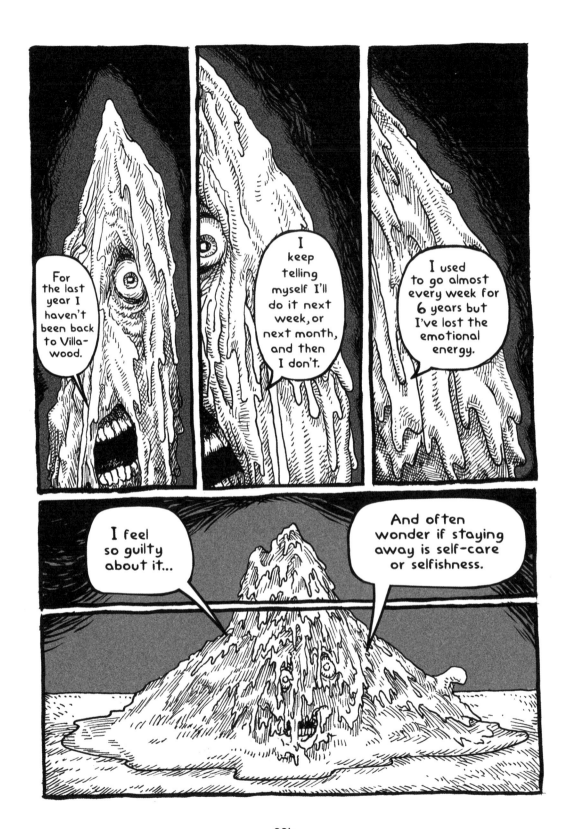

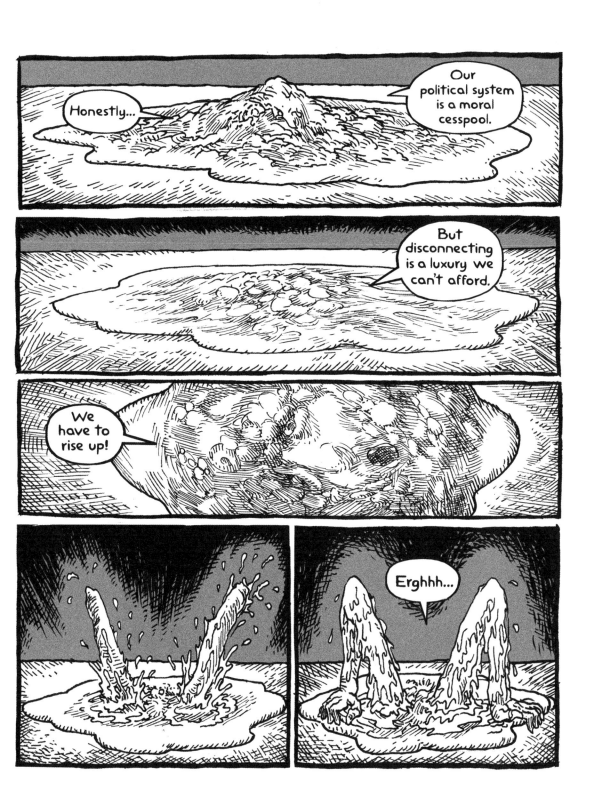

225

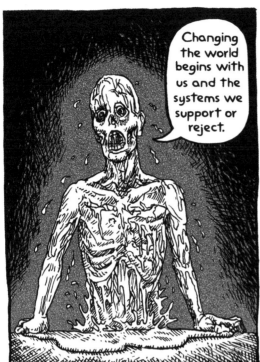

Which is sometimes as simple as it sounds.

# Afterword

*Still Alive* was created on the traditional lands of the Guringai, Darug, Gandangara, Gadigal and Wangal peoples of what we call Sydney. I acknowledge their Elders past and present, recognising that sovereignty was never ceded.

This graphic novel began in 2015 as a web-comic called *Villawood: Notes from an immigration detention centre*. That comic was made for the advocacy organisation GetUp!, with support from a crowdsourcing venture aimed at funding alternative journalism on the refugee issue. Later that year the lovely people at Twelve Panels Press asked if I would adapt it for print publication.

However, the actual genesis of this book goes back a decade, when I started visiting the Villawood Immigration Detention Centre with some friends. Through these visits, we founded a small, not-for-profit community art organisation, Refugee Art Project, for which I still volunteer. Some of that experience is depicted in this book, including artworks made in the Villawood Immigration Detention Centre by refugees who were then detained. Refugee Art Project has fostered some wonderful friendships and a strong sense of community over many years. It is the wellspring of the stories and collaborations that make up this work. To everyone who trusted me with their testimony, wrapped in hours of hospitality, conversation and patience, I am deeply grateful.

I would also like to thank those friends who offered crucial feedback and reflection, not to mention tons of much-needed emotional support. They include Can Yalcinkaya, Zeinab Mirabadi, Susan Nelson, Cecily Niumeitolu, Pat Grant, Zeina Iaali, Bilquis Ghani, Michael Fikaris, Sam Wallman, Agnieszka Switala, Anton Pulvirenti, Ted McKinley, Daniella Trimboli, Eleni Xristou, Jose

Galarza, Kim Gogan, Josie Barron, Margaret Mejhju, Paula Abood, Moones Mansoubi, Thomas Wales, Lisa Worthington and Anjali Vishwanathan. I am grateful to Erica Wagner, Bernard Caleo and Elizabeth MacFarlane, my wonderful publishers at Twelve Panels Press, for all their careful editorial guidance, proofreading and encouragement. And to my friends who lent their expertise in human rights law or medicine, Rawan Andalus, Daniel Ghezelbash, Jonathan Phillips, Marissa Ram, Ryan Essex and all the brave whistleblowers who have brought the Australian government's injustices to light. Special thanks go to my loving and supportive family, Anna Broom, Syed Nazeer Ahmed, Farukh Jabeen Ahmed, Iqbal, Zehra and Samara.

I dedicate this book to my dear friend, Ahmad Ali Jafari, who died of a heart attack inside the Villawood Immigration Detention Centre in June 2013. I commit it to everyone who has suffered as a result of Australia's cruel border policies, their families, friends and communities.

# Where they are now

Of the people featured in this comic only Saad Tlaa is living with his family and rebuilding his life as an Australian citizen. At the time of writing (November 2020), the rest are living in the community on temporary visas of three or five years' duration which were imposed on people who travelled to Australia by boat. Despite all of them being recognised as refugees, they are unable to attain citizenship or bring their families to Australia, which in many cases includes the limbo of partners and children who wait in their country of origin or in third countries.

# Further Reading

Here's a short list of informative resources about refugee issues in Australia:

Jane McAdam, *Refugee Rights and Policy Wrongs*, UNSW Press, 2019

Behrouz Boochani, *No Friend but the Mountains*, Picador, 2018

Daniel Ghezelbash, *Refuge Lost: Asylum Law in an Interdependent World*, Cambridge University Press, 2018

Professors Suvendrini Perera & Joseph Pugliese, *Deathscapes: Mapping Race and Violence in Settler States*, Macquarie University, 2016–2020

William Maley, *What is a Refugee?*, C Hurst & Co Publishers Ltd, 2016

Susan Metcalfe, *The Pacific Solution*, Australian Scholarly Publishing, 2010

David Marr and Marian Wilkinson, *Dark Victory*, Allen & Unwin, 2004

# What can I do?

Please consider supporting or joining with refugee-led organisations or other bodies which offer important legal or practical support to refugees in the Australian community: RISE: Refugees, Survivors and Ex-detainees, Refugee Voices, RACS Refugee Advice & Casework Service, Asylum Seekers Centre, Australian Centre for International Justice, Refugee Council of Australia.

There are many important creative communities involving people of an asylum seeker or refugee background, including: Writing Through Fences, the Refugee Welcome Centre at Callan Park Sydney, MAFA: Melbourne Artists for Asylum Seekers, Third Space and Refugee Art Project.

Beyond supporting the above organisations it is important to vote thoughtfully, boycott companies which profit from the detention industry, protest in the streets and write letters to local politicians.

*'The refugee movement is the movement of the 21st century. It's the movement that is challenging the effects of global capitalism, it's the movement that is calling for civil rights for all human beings.'*

Angela Davis, renowned human rights advocate, while visiting a refugee-occupied school in Germany in May 2015.

Safdar Ahmed is a Sydney-based artist, musician and educator. He is a founding member of the community art organisation Refugee Art Project, and member of eleven, a collective of contemporary Muslim Australian artists, curators and writers. He is the author of *Reform and Modernity in Islam* (IB Tauris, 2013) and the Walkley Award–winning documentary webcomic *Villawood: Notes from an immigration detention centre* (2015). He also sings and plays guitar with the anti-racist death metal band Hazeen.